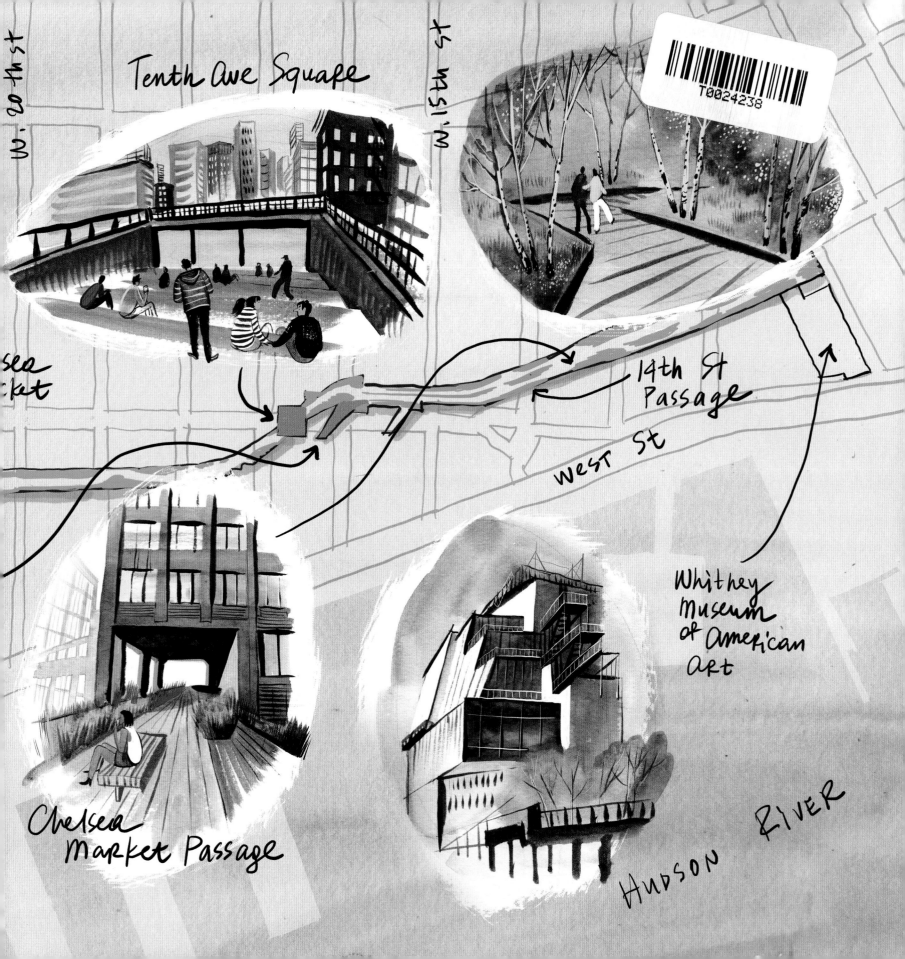

W. 20th st

Tenth Ave Square

W. 15th st

14th St
Passage

West St

...sea
...ket

Whitney
Museum
of American
Art

Chelsea
Market Passage

HUDSON RIVER

To my parents, who instilled the love of cities and architecture in me.
To Alex and Jacob, who, I hope, inherited this love. And to the city of
New York, my ever-changing and constant inspiration.

The illustrations for this book were created with watercolor and digitally.

Cataloging-in-Publication Data has been applied for and may be obtained from the Library of Congress.

ISBN 978-1-4197-5670-2

Text and illustrations © 2023 Victoria Tentler-Krylov
Edited by Howard W. Reeves
Book design by Heather Kelly

Printed and bound in China
10 9 8 7 6 5 4 3 2 1

Abrams Books for Young Readers are available at special discounts when purchased in quantity
for premiums and promotions as well as fundraising or educational use. Special editions can also be created to specification.
For details, contact specialsales@abramsbooks.com or the address below.

ABRAMS The Art of Books
195 Broadway, New York, NY 10007
abramsbooks.com

The HIGH LINE

A PARK TO LOOK UP TO

VICTORIA TENTLER-KRYLOV

Abrams Books for Young Readers

New York

A long, clanging train, blowing its horn, barreled along the tracks through the streets of New York City. Its destination was a big factory on the West Side. The train was loud and dirty, but the people of the City needed it: It carried countless bags of flour, crates of coal, and cisterns of milk to the factories that baked bread and packaged meat and milk.

The City had an idea: to raise the railroad tracks above the streets. Now the trains rolled above people's heads. They were still loud and dirty, but they didn't endanger people or block traffic anymore. The trains rolled right into huge second-floor windows of factories and warehouses. There, workers hustled to unload and reload the boxes, crates, and packages.

After a while, horse buggies gave way to automobiles. Now huge freight trucks carried their loads into the factories at the street level, where workers continued to unload and load them.

Fewer and fewer trains rolled on the overhead tracks. The ones that still did were getting shorter. Sometimes, weeks would go by without the clanging and the whistles. A few grassy patches spread over the crossties. The grass grew taller and taller.

The City decided the time had come to close off the elevated tracks. Before Thanksgiving one year, the last train rolled through, carrying turkeys.

As time went by, the grassy areas grew together to form a meadow, and wildflowers and young trees swayed in the wind. In the winter, falling snow muffled the sounds of the traffic below and turned the green field into a blanket of white. High above the rushing people and the traffic jams, it was a different world: a constantly changing, silent, forgotten world in the sky.

A group of neighbors kept looking up at the abandoned tracks. *Surely they could be used for something*, they said. But what? They brainstormed ideas and new names for the elevated railroad. They decided to call it the High Line, and to call themselves Friends of the High Line.

There was just one problem: The City thought the tracks were useless and falling apart. Friends of the High Line were told, "The High Line will be dismantled and removed."

But the neighbors knew about the secret world in the sky, about the wildflowers and the trees. The shop owners, gas station workers, residents, artists, and architects gathered together and decided they had to find a new use for the High Line. They had to convince the City to keep it!

The Friends imagined the future: Trees and flowers would bloom overhead, and new cafés and art galleries would sprout on the streets below. Parents, children, students, the young and old alike, whether alone or together, everyone from all over the City would come to enjoy it. Maybe even from other cities. Or other countries!

The City was intrigued. *Let's give it a try*, it said.

The Friends called for a competition of ideas. When artists and architects learned about it, they let their imaginations run wild.

Mile-long Lap Pool for Swimming and Boating!

Suggestions and ideas poured in from people all over the world, each one crazier than the next.

Huge Roller Coaster!

A Bench Trolley That Rolls on the Tracks!

The winning idea didn't have roller coasters or swimming pools, but it had something other ideas didn't.

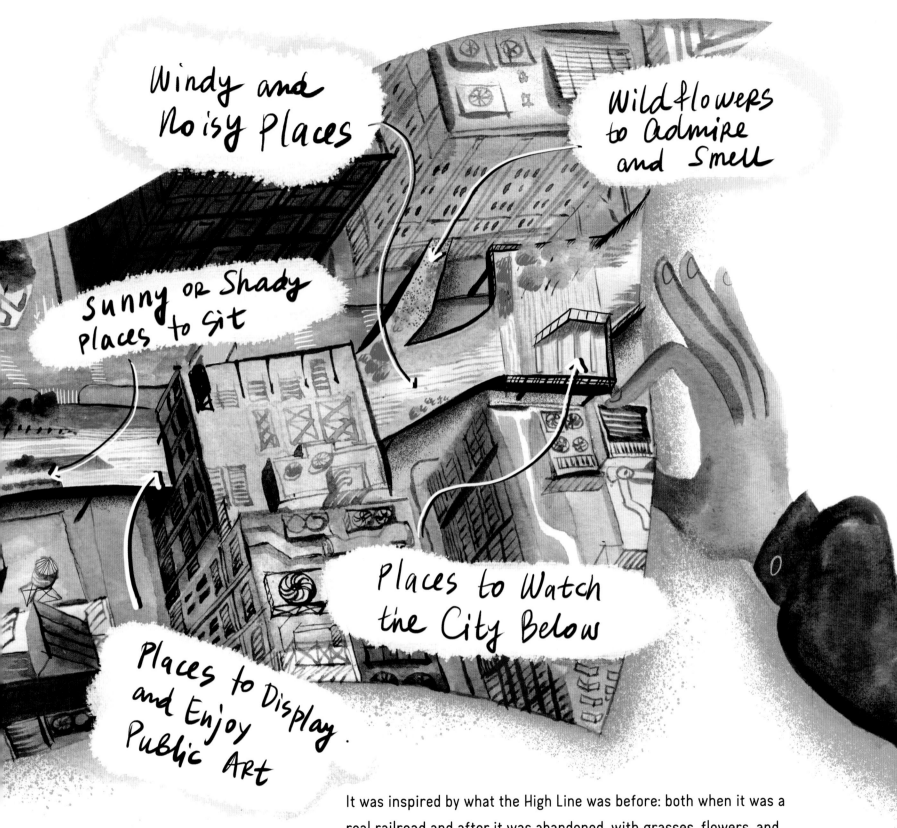

It was inspired by what the High Line was before: both when it was a real railroad and after it was abandoned, with grasses, flowers, and trees growing wild between the tracks.

The City decided to build just a short section first.

When it opened, visitors flooded the park, marveling at the lush greenery and the views of the City from new angles. The High Line weaved between buildings like a suspended green river.

People glided along the paths as if in a dream. When they reached the fence at the end of the section, they frowned.

They wanted more!

The City had good news to share. The next section was already being built!
It was clear how important the park was becoming. It wasn't just
a nice green place to enjoy a sunny day. It was a destination for New
Yorkers and visitors alike.

The park was now so popular that it spread excitement and energy far beyond its own boundaries. There was even a name for this: the "High Line effect." New shops, cafés, and even a museum were sprouting up all along the High Line as more and more people flocked to the neighborhood.

But life was getting harder for those who had lived there for years before. Their favorite bodegas and butcher shops were gone. Everything was too shiny and too crowded. The neighborhood didn't feel like their home anymore, and they worried if they could stay.

As the High Line grew longer section by section, people from all over the world continued to come. They walked along the paths and gazed at the City below. They touched the trees and lay on the grass, staring up at the sky.

The visitors left feeling energetic and inspired.

But the longtime residents needed the High Line to still feel like their home park as well. They came up with ideas: to open the park to live music and neighborhood dance parties and to invite local artists to share their art. They talked about how the High Line could help improve the life in the local neighborhoods.
They talked about the future.

London

Washington, D.C.

Chicago

Mexico City

As word about the High Line spread, something started happening all over the world. Other cities were now looking at their own abandoned rail lines, tram tracks, or viaducts. They began to develop plans to turn these spaces into new urban parks.

The High Line's organizers and community joined together to help these cities. They saw each new project as an extension of the High Line, and as a chance to reinvent it. They started to work with the longtime neighbors to come up with ideas for how these new public spaces could help improve their lives.

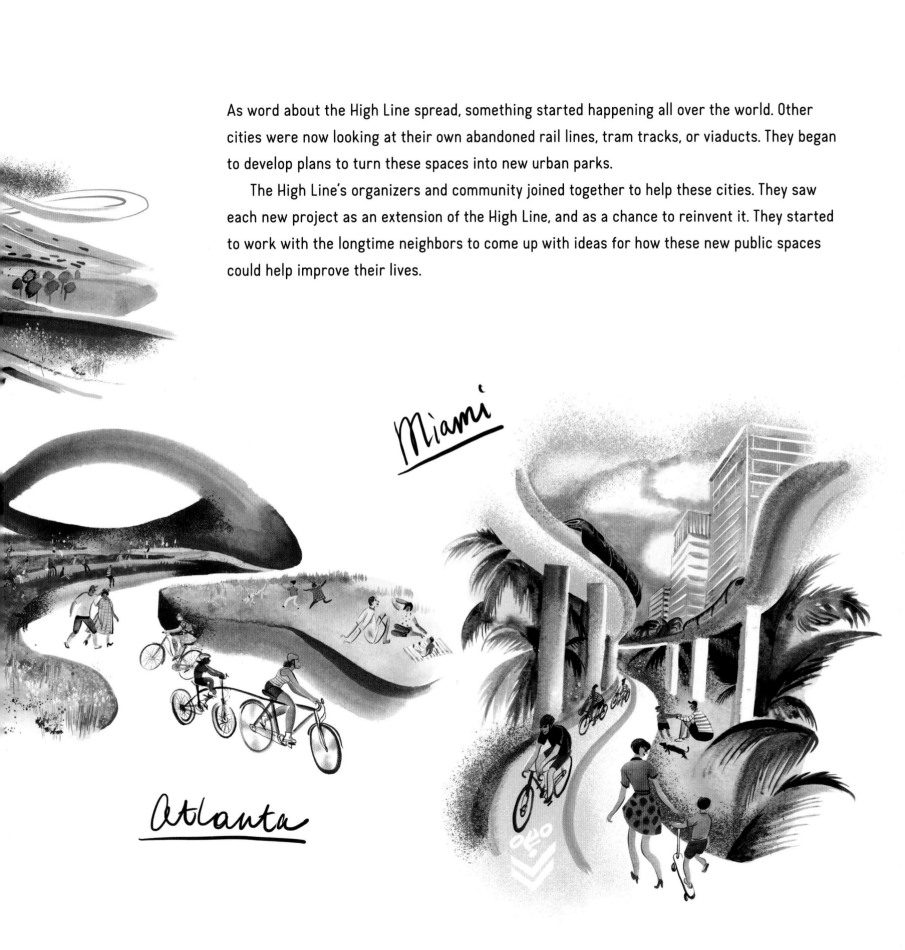

Miami

Atlanta

Today, the story of the High Line continues over the world.
It's a story that's being told in many places and by many people.
And as people continue to rethink it, learn from it, and help it
evolve, the park keeps getting better with each chapter.

AUTHOR'S NOTE

My first memory of the High Line is from before it became the High Line as we know it today.

I went to architecture school in New York, and my classmates and I loved to explore the city, looking for the "undiscovered" spots in the midst of the urban hustle and bustle. We wandered around all five boroughs, sketching, taking endless photos, admiring the beauty of the abandoned warehouses, docks, and factories. One day, somewhere in Chelsea, we discovered a rickety metal ladder leading up to the forgotten train tracks above our heads. The sidewalk was full of people, but we seemed to be the only ones who noticed the ladder. We did not hesitate to climb up. It was like entering Narnia: Grasses and wildflowers swayed, trees rustled, butterflies fluttered. Incredible panoramas of the river and the streets below unfolded just for us. It was quiet, mysterious, even a little dangerous. It was the most unique place we'd seen. We couldn't stop talking about how it could be brought back to life and shared with the community.

Soon after, we learned about the plans for the High Line redevelopment. We followed the design updates, watched construction unfold, then watched the park fill up with people. The secret world we thought belonged just to us was not secret anymore—now it belonged to everyone. Within a space of a few years, its popularity became overwhelming. The gritty blocks along the High Line transformed, too, filling up with shiny condo buildings, boutiques, and restaurants. By all these measures, the High Line was an incredible, indisputable success.

But was it as simple as that? The original neighborhoods held affordable businesses and low-income housing, where many residents were people of color. Was the High Line serving them, too? In the crush of new visitors, many locals felt lost or pushed away. Could the High Line create jobs, help the local community, perhaps even lower housing costs for the longtime neighbors? Could it have become an inclusive neighborhood park that the community could use as its own? Friends of the High Line agreed that it could have, if the right questions had been asked and if the community had had more input into the design from the get-go.

But there were still ways to engage local residents, and to use the High Line to help its neighbors. Friends of the High Line launched job training and education programs for local kids. They started arts and music programs to showcase local artists. They worked in partnership with the neighbors to create events just for them. Perhaps even more important, they founded the High Line Network, a group of future public-space projects nationwide that had one goal in common: to serve as many people as possible and to help the communities around them.

The park's organizers began to share their findings and realizations. Now they are helping others create more inclusive environments that serve the community, improve the lives of local residents, and engage those who need them most.

The High Line's evolution, though stunning, is more complicated than it seems. But as an architect, I can't help but get excited about each new project following in the High Line's footsteps. What is a community park? What is public space? How do we make it inclusive? Every new project gives us a new opportunity to learn from the mistakes of its predecessors and answer these questions in its own way.

I can't wait to see them succeed.

A BRIEF HIGH LINE TIMELINE

Mid-1800s to 1920s: The freight trains of the New York Central Railroad run on street level, endangering people and horses. To protect pedestrians, the "West Side Cowboys" ride in front of the trains, waving flags and yelling warnings to get out of the way.

1930s: New York City's Transit Commission removes street-level crossings and builds elevated tracks that run through buildings and branch out into factories above street level. The trains deliver millions of tons of meat, dairy, and produce directly into the factories without disturbing the streets below.

1960s: As trucking begins to develop in the United States, the use of freight trains gradually declines.

1980s: The railroad sits unused and begins to break down in some areas. Many people begin to call for removal of the tracks, calling them an ugly eyesore.

1990s: Joshua David and Robert Hammond found Friends of the High Line, a nonprofit group dedicated to the preservation and redevelopment of the tracks.

2003: Friends of the High Line announce an "ideas competition" to raise awareness of the project that results in hundreds of proposals from all over the world.

2004–2006: The architectural firm of Diller Scofidio + Renfro is chosen as the winner. Plans get underway to start the first phase of the project.

2009: The first section of the High Line, from Gansevoort Street to 20th Street, opens to the public. Construction of the second section begins.

2011: The second section, from 20th to 30th Street, opens.

2014: The High Line at the Rail Yards, from 30th to 34th Streets, opens.

2021: A proposal to extend the High Line further east and north is announced.

2022: Groundbreaking is held in February for the High Line connection to Moynihan Train Hall, starting at 30th Street and Tenth Avenue.

SELECTED BIBLIOGRAPHY

Bendov, Pavel, and Alexandra Lange. *New Architecture New York*. New York: Prestel, 2017.

Corner, James. *The High Line*. New York: Phaidon Press, 2020.

David, Joshua, and Robert Hammond. *High Line: The Inside Story of New York City's Park in the Sky*. New York: FSG Originals, 2011.

"The Freight Yard." Vintage rail film of New York Central Railroad (archival video). See www.youtube.com/watch?v=4SfcJ8BFx-8.

Higgins, Adrian. "The High Line has been sidelined. When it reopens, New Yorkers may get the park they always wanted." *Washington Post*, June 24, 2020. See www.washingtonpost.com/lifestyle/home/the-high-line-has-been-sidelined-when-it-reopens-new-yorkers-may-get-the-park-they-always-wanted/2020/06/23/5e2a59e0-acd1-11ea-94d2-d7bc43b26bf9_story.html.

The High Line (official website). See www.thehighline.org.

High Line Network. See network.thehighline.org/about.

New York Central System Historical Society. See nycshs.blogspot.com/2008/05/nyc-railroad-history.html.

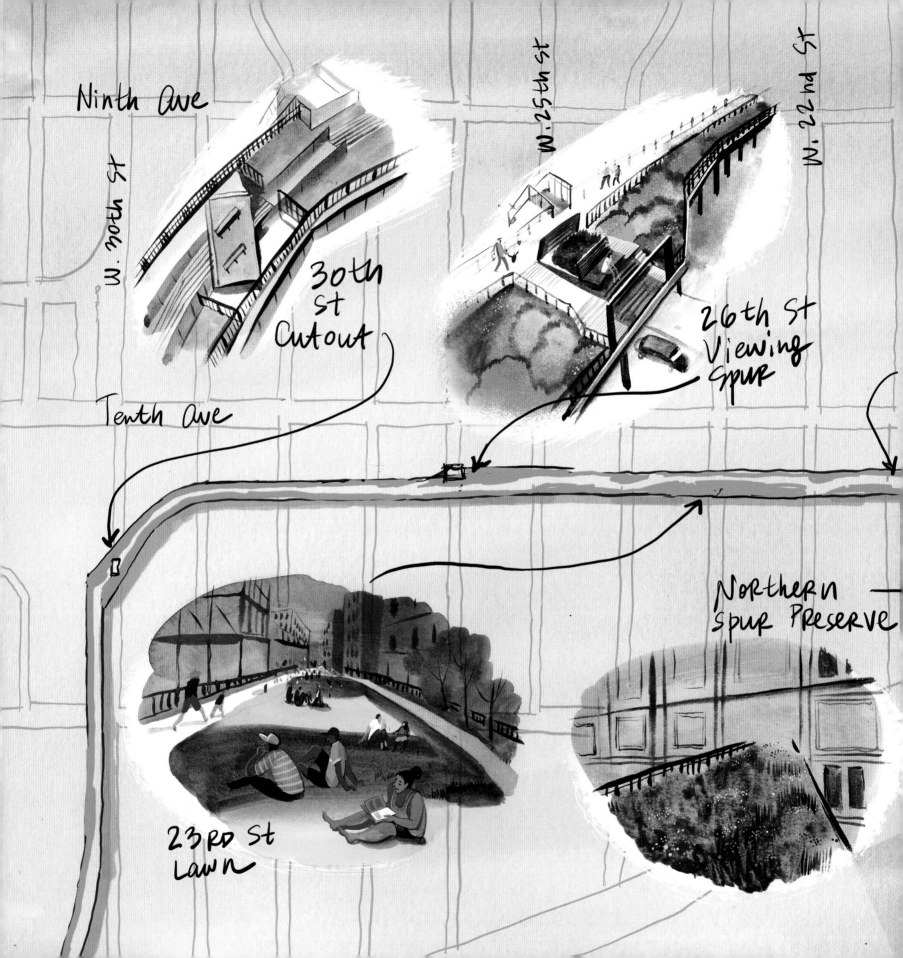

Ninth Ave

W. 30th St

Tenth Ave

W. 25th St

W. 22nd St

30th St Cutout

26th St Viewing Spur

Northern Spur Preserve

23RD St Lawn